STRENGTH TRAINING OF THE EASTERN BLOC - POWERLIFTING

TABLE OF CONTENTS

STRENGTH TRAINING OF THE EASTERN BLOC - POWERLIFTING	3
BASICS	4
THE GENERAL ADAPTATION SYNDROME	4
PRINCIPLE SPECIFICATION	4
PRINCIPLE OF FATIGUE MANAGEMENT	6
SUMMARY	7
VOLUME, FREQUENCY, INTENSITY	8
INTENSITY	9
INTENSITY AND SPECIFICATION	10
INTENSITY AND MUSCLE GROWTH	10
VOLUME	11
INTRODUCTION TO FREQUENCY	12
VOLUME AND FREQUENCY	14
THE HIGH VOLUME TRAP	14
OPTIMUM FREQUENCY	15
PERIODIZATION BEGINNER, ADVANCED, ELITE	16
MICROCYCLE AND MESOCYCLE	18
PRILEPIN TABLE	21
RUSSIAN COMPLEX SENTENCES	24
SHEIKO ROUTINE	27
SMOLOV SQUAT CYCLE	33
EXTENDED RUSSIAN POWER ROUTINE 9 WEEKS	40
BULGARIAN METHOD FOR POWERLIFTING	45

Strength Training of the Eastern Bloc - Powerlifting

Foreword.

This book should give you a little theory and overview of Russian training plans and the Eastern bloc.

Fundamentals of theory and analysis of plans in strength training.

For many more useful information, then visit https://www.powerliftingcheck.de

BASICS

With this series I will be going through some points, with which one can rate a training plan.

THE GENERAL ADAPTATION SYNDROME

Now what does that mean? It is the theory of stress-recovery-adjustment behavior. So the stress refers to the training stimulus you have set. Here, the body is now something "destroyed" or release toxins. Now the dose of the stimulus must be high enough to be considered as a burden and enough "damage" to supply. The body must now repair these damages. What is called recovery. This recovery can be influenced by appropriate nutrition and supplements and therefore also accelerate. After repair, the body will now adapt to better prepare for further stimuli. So, to get less damage from the same stimulus.

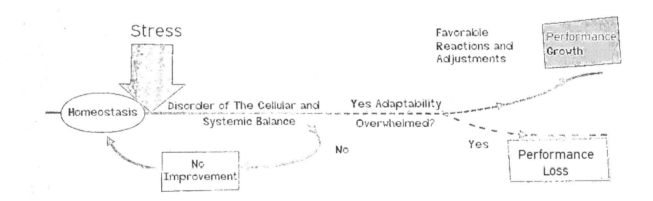

As an example: A cellar child goes into the sun and gets sunburn. Now the skin will recover and turn a little brown. Now the cellar child can stay out longer and does not get the next sunburn quite fast.

What does that mean for us? After every stimulus and complete recovery, we must increase the next stimulus. So move more weights from workout to workout.

PRINCIPLE SPECIFICATION

Following the general adjustment syndrome pattern, we now need to perform heavy squats, heavy bench presses, and heavy deadlifts as the powerlifter at the appropriate frequency.

The division of repetitions helps us to do this.

1-5 reps for power

5-10 repetitions for muscle

10-25 repetitions for stamina

One thing must be noted though. With 3 repetitions you will also build muscle. The transition is fluid.

The law of accommodation "law of accommodation" states that the more often the body is exposed to the same stimulus, the less the body will show adaptive response (adaptation). This applies to a large extent to the choice of movement and to a lesser extent to the training intensity.

Let's take the squat. In the first training you will get 100% as return on investment. The 2nd training maybe 80%, the 3rd 60% and the 4th training maybe 40%. Well, if, for example, a paused squat is done, then the carry will be 75%. This means that if you use paused squat as 3rd training, you will end up with more carry over or more adjustment. Thus, get more results for the time invested.

Principle overload

Following the pattern of the general adaptation syndrome, we have to overload the body again and again. So always new stimuli with a higher dose. We can with this.

More weight

More sentences

More repetitions

Or slightly modified exercises (example paused squat)

Means we must do more and more in the course of our powerlifting career!

Also in powerlifting, if you do not do something, or do not train, then you will lose it slowly.

PRINCIPLE OF FATIGUE MANAGEMENT

It is important to understand this principle. The higher the stress on your recovery capacity, the longer the recovery will take.

So your appeal is too high and the next day of training too early, then you will slowly lose weight physically because you train too much. If your training stimulus is too small and the break between days is too long, you will also lose weight physically. So remember. Timing is important here! (timed coordination)

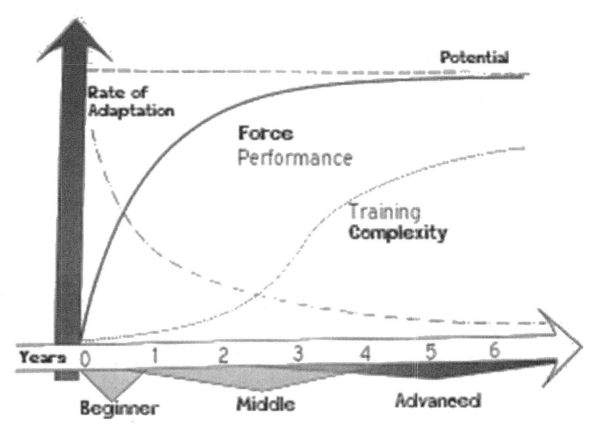

Principle individual differences

Many training programs ignore the law of individual differences. Not every body reacts immediately to the stimuli and volume. For example, some need 5 sets more squat to make progress than other people.

Not everyone can handle the same job.

Biomechanical conditions also influence the training and progress. By way of example, longer legs alter the leverage and, accordingly, adjustments need to be made, which muscles you train more to force further progress.

SUMMARY

General Adjustment syndrome and Restoration of the supercompensation

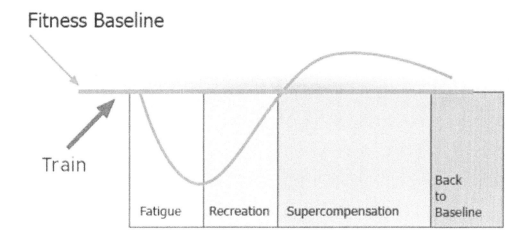

The following points must be looked at to see if a training plan is good.

specification

There must be a lot of heavy squat, heavy bench press and heavy deadlift.

overload

You have to constantly overload your body with more weight, repetitions or sets. No new stimuli, no new adjustments.

fatigue management

Temporal coordination of workouts is important. If the stimulus is too high and there is not enough rest, you will probably get into overtraining and break down. If the stimuli are too small and the breaks too long, then you come into the lower training and will dismantle or stay the same.

individual differences

A plan should be set to your own differences. Each body needs a different dose of stimuli, exercises or volume. Also in view of biomechanics.

VOLUME, FREQUENCY, INTENSITY

Now let's talk about variables that we can modify perfectly. That's volume, frequency and intensity.

Intensity

The intensity is one of the most important factors. This does not refer to how hard you try, but how heavy the weights are in relation to your maximum weight. For example: You can move Max in the squat 100 kilos exactly once. Now a set of 80 kilos is made, which now corresponds to 80% intensity.

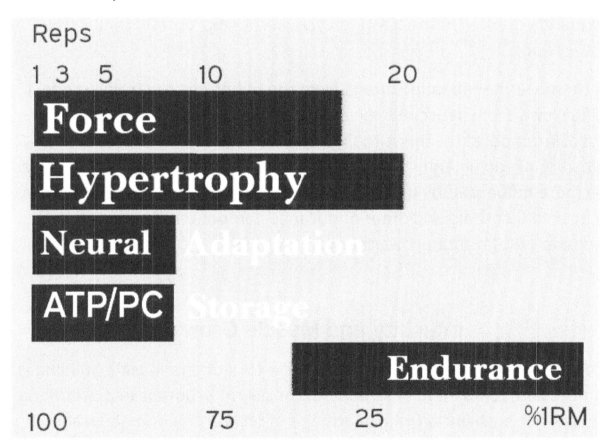

Intensity and Specification

Training in the 90% + range, which corresponds to 1 to 3 repetitions, the training effect will be primarily neural in nature. Simply put, your nervous system will improve its overall efficiency through the maximum levels of muscle compartment. In addition, the coordination of this compartment will improve, leading to further performance improvements.

A huge part of the power used in moving a maximum weight will be neuronal in nature. In order for a program to be able to meet the specification threshold for powerlifting training, you must train frequently or often in the training cycle at the appropriate time in the 90% + range.

As we move the repeating image from top to bottom, the training effect shifts slowly from neuronal efficiency to muscle-building and then muscular endurance. This is mainly due to the fact that low repetition rates are predominantly restricted by force, while higher repetition rates are more influenced by metabolic fatigue factors such as ATP depletion, lactic acid threshold and other endurance components that are not necessarily relevant to powerlifting.

Intensity and Muscle Growth

Probably not less than 75% with only a few exceptions. Muscle building is a necessary component of sustained, consistent progress in powerlifting. You cannot push out an infinite amount of technology and general neural efficiency. At some point you need a bigger engine to drive faster and further. In a good powerlifting program, a lifter will spend time in the 75-85% intensity range. This corresponds to sets of 4-8 repetitions and builds up a larger musculature.

You get what you train. If your training consists of nothing but sets of 5, you will get a nice mix of strength and size. However, 5s are optimal neither for strength nor size. So, spending some time in this area is beneficial but spending solely on this area would make a program non-specific to powerlifting. You have to train hard.

Remember, intensity determines training effect. For powerlifting we want the training effect to be an increase in maximum power production and that involves very heavy weights.

Volume

To quote Mike Tuchscherer, *"when the intensity determines the training effect, the volume determines the size of that effect".*

For example, if you expose your skin to sunlight, you will probably get a tan ("a training effect"). If you stay in the sun for a minute, you might not have done enough to provide adequate "stress." The body must not be forced to compensate because you have not overloaded it. If you stay in the sun for two hours, you will get a lot of "stress", but it will probably be too much and you will probably burn. Both are not a good result.

More importantly, there are a wide range of possibilities in the middle. If you spend 15 minutes in the sun, you will get a degree of tanning; If you spend 30 minutes in the sun, you will get another level of tanning. In this case, the time in the sun is our "volume" of stress and the level of tanning is the "size" of the training effect.

In training, we can define the volume in a variety of ways: the number of total reps in a workout, the number of sets, or we can calculate "tonnage." Tonnage is nothing more than the calculation of the total repetitions and sets that you have moved through the weight. For example, if you squat 100x5x5, then you have accumulated (100 * 5 * 5 =) 2500 kilos as total tonnage.

The more tonnage accumulated, the greater the training effect will be. But that also determines the longer you have to wait before you can train again. As with everyone, there is an optimal dose-response relationship.

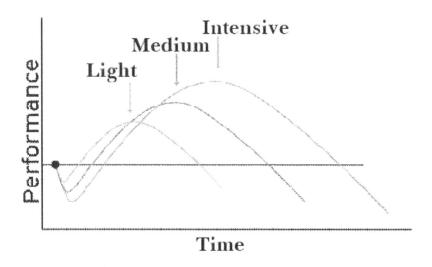

Introduction to Frequency

Frequency simply means how often each discipline is trained. For example, if you work bench press 3 times a week, your frequency for this exercise is exactly 3.

Frequency is very important in terms of recreation management. If you train too often and do not recover enough, then you get into overtraining. If you do not train enough, the body will not make any adjustments and you will not make any progress here either. With both mistakes, the performance will suffer, so it is important to have good time coordination for these two processes.

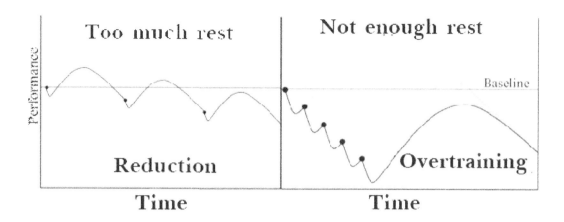

The goal of temporal coordination should be to set another stimulus (stress) at the right time, so that the body must readjust and progress.

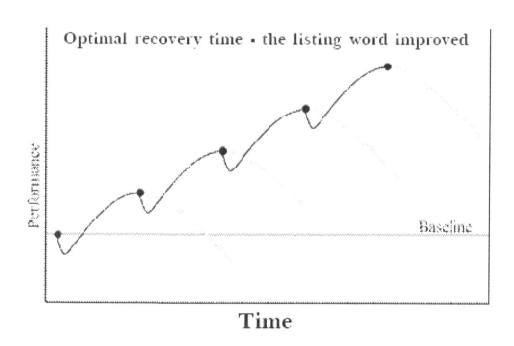

Volume and Frequency

Now we know that a lot of volume during training session needs more time for recovery. So we have to train with less frequency. If you train less volume, you should increase the frequency.

Now the question is: what is the optimal dose?

The relationship between volume and training effect is not straight. Extra volume does not bring the same increase in maximum weight. For example, hypothetically, let's say you know that 205x5x5 will increase the maximum weight by 5 kilos. 205x5x10 does not increase your maximum weight by 10 kilos, even though the volume is twice that. You might get around 7.5 kilos.

The High Volume Trap

Now if more volume produces more training effect, why not train like that? So, what do we have to do to get more adaptation to the stimulus? Your reply is more volume over time. Well, training 200x5x10 (reps x sets) from the beginning will take a tremendous amount of time, energy, and willingness, and since most power-lifters are not professional athletes, they simply do not have the time for several hours every single day work out.

Secondly, the body must first get used to such a high volume. If you jump directly to such a high volume, then you have simply made fewer stress-relaxation adjustment cycles than someone who has been working slowly.

For clear understanding, your competitor will beat you at 200x5x10 by 7.5 pounds, compared to yours at 200x5x5 and 5 pounds. But by the time you have worked your way up to 5 × 10, you will make 5 × 5 more 5 kilos jumps than the one who makes 7.5 kilos.

Optimum Frequency

This frequency is thus determined by the volume that you make on a training day and can recover from it, thereby creating an adjustment. Your frequency could be something like twice a week. However, at some point, you will reach the point where you have to put so much volume into a training day that you spend more than 3-4 hours in the studio to make progress. Now it would probably be time to increase the frequency and divide the volume.

The key is to note the recovery time as well as to do the next workout where the physical performance is at maximum.

PERIODIZATION BEGINNER, ADVANCED, ELITE

Firstly, we must define what is necessary for a correct periodization.

1. Plan the calendar year. When is the next competition? How many weeks are necessary or available. Analyze strengths and weaknesses.

2. Organization of training goals. For example, in early exercise months the focus on muscle building.

3. Planning of microcycles with manipulation of frequency, volume and intensity. Which exercises have to be chosen. Everything with the background of the year planning.

Beginner

A beginner is someone who can recover from training to training and can further improvee. In the sense of stress-recovery-adjustment cycle. As an example, a novice on Monday can do a best in deadlift and improve on Wednesday.

Beginners need to improve strength, muscles and technique at the same time.

This is called the complex-parallel approach.

Now it makes no sense for a beginner to choose the periodization so that different training blocks are created with different focus. Beginners need very little volume to progress. With the background, beginners can simultaneously train all training goals without jeopardizing their capacity to adapt.

In reality, a beginner does not need manipulation of volume and intensity. Optimal volume is easy to set enough stimuli for each workout to get an adjustment and not so much that you can not recover enough. Volume changes are not necessary.

Because a beginner is so easily able to improve all physical attributes, it makes a lot of sense to choose an intensity range of 80 to 85%. This area has a nice mix of muscle gain, technique enhancement and strength enhancement. Mostly sentences with 5 repetitions are used for it.

Advanced

As an advanced one is someone who can no longer improve from training to training.

The advanced must put a stimulus to further adaptation, which needs more time to recover. (48 to 72 hours). This means that volume and intensity must now be manipulated.

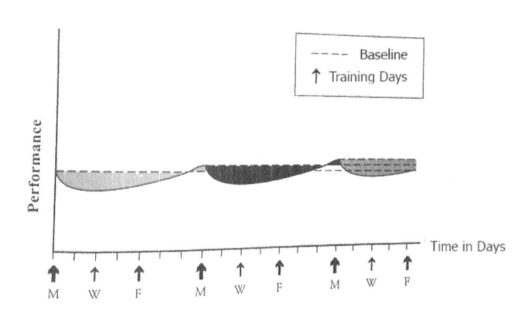

As an example, the Texas Method

Monday: 5 × 5 squat

Wednesday: slight 2 × 5 squat

Friday: 5 repetitions with maximum weight

A volume training day followed by a light day to improve recovery and prevent performance degradation. On Friday, the athlete will try to get the best performance to see his performance improvements. Every week the cycle is repeated.

Nevertheless, the complex-parallel approach is perfectly appropriate in terms of periodization. Advanced users usually do not require specific concentrations for individual performance characteristics. Programming diversity and load manipulation is all that is needed to get progress.

MICROCYCLE AND MESOCYCLE

At this point, I have to introduce the concepts of mesocycles and microcycles. For the beginner, each workout and the following recovery period represents both a full mesocycle and a microcycle. With the weekly Texas Method model discussed above, Monday, Wednesday, and Friday would represent all microcycles, each with an individual purpose, and Each training week would represent a complete training mesocycle.

Mon: volume day - microcycle

Mi: day of rest - microcycle

Fr: intensity day - microcycle

Every full week of training: mesocycle

You can easily see how the "Texas Method" model could be applied to a three-week wave instead of being held within a single week. In this case, each week with its particular combination of volumes and intensities would represent a microcycle and the full three weeks would be a mesocycle.

Week 1: Volume Week / "Accumulation" - microcycle

Week 2: Recovery week / Deload microcycle

Week 3: Intensity Week / "Intensification" - microcycle

Every three-week wave: mesocycle

Elite

Finally, an athlete will reach the point where the volumes required to stimulate further improvements in certain physical attributes are so high that it becomes physically impossible to evolve them at the same time.

While it is true that the work capacity and the recovery capacity improve in the course of an athlete's training career, they do so absolutely. There is an upper limit to recovery for everyone. When this point is reached, an athlete will risk coming into overtraining if they continue to train after the complex-parallel approach.

Now what follows is called block periodization. Block periodization uses scheduled training periods or mesocycles to focus on specific physical attributes such as muscle hypertrophy, maximum strength or explosive strength. In each block, only the focus is placed on an attribute. The blocks are organized in strategic order so that the effects of the previous block in the next positively influence.

Pendulum / Emphasis periodization scheme

So, at one end of the spectrum, we have complex parallel periodization, where practically all physical attributes are trained simultaneously, and on the other hand, we have block periodization, where each quality is trained in isolation. As you may have already realized, the reality is that the vast majority of us will benefit most from something between the two extremes.

A very smart approach is the pendulum / emphasis periodization scheme. In low season, for example, 67% of our training may be focused on muscle hypertrophy, while only 33% would focus on improving maximum power production. For "early" advanced trainees (remember, it is a continuum), this will result in small improvements in maximum strength and high gains in muscle hypertrophy. As the training cycle progresses, the pendulum would swing and the emphasis can become 67% of maximum power production. In this way, multiple physical attributes are improved simultaneously, but the load is concentrated in a particular direction.

It is my belief that this pendulum / emphasis style of periodization will be optimal for most powerlifters with years of training experience.

Summary

Whenever we organize our training, the first thing we have to consider is the competition plan. When is the next competition? How many weeks do we have? What level of an athlete do we have?

If we are a "beginner", very little planning and training is required for variable manipulation. The beginner can use a complex parallel periodization, improve all important training qualities at the same time and work without diversity in intensity and volume from training to training.

Well, if we are an "advanced", by definition, we will require variation from microcycle to microcycle in terms of intensity and volume. Typically, intermediate programs require periods of "accumulation" (higher volume) and "intensification" (low volumes, but heavy weights). The length of accumulation and intensification depends on the exact adaptability of the athlete. They could operate within a weekly mesocycle like the Texas Method, or they could use a monthly mesocycle like Jim Wendler's 5/3/1.

Only elites require more complex periodization models. For the elite athlete, the volumes required to achieve progress in any given physical attribute are so high that it is simply impossible to develop them all at the same time. As such, times with a focus on specific attributes become necessary, and this is where block periodization enters the image. Not only does the elite athlete have to integrate complex programming models that adequately manipulate volume and intensity.

	Mesocycle 1	Mesocycle 2	Mesocycle 3
Beginners Periodization Focus Programming	All Attributes	All Attributes	All Attributes
	Static	Static	Static
Advanced Periodization Focus Programming	Mesocycle 1	Mesocycle 2	Mesozyklus 3
	All Attributes	All Attributes	All Attributes
	High volume, Medium Intensity	Low Volume, Medium Intensity	Medium Volume, High Intensity
Elite Periodization Focus Programming	Mesocycle 1	Mesocycle 2	Mesocycle 3
	Muscle Growth	Speed	Force
	High Volume, Medium Intensity	Low Volume, Medium Intensity	Medium Volume, High Intensity

PRILEPIN TABLE

The following questions should be answered here.

What does the Prilepin table look like? What is the purpose of the Prilepin table? How to apply the Prilepin table for different intensity ranges? Who invented the Prilepin Table?

What does the Prilepin table look like?

Intensity	Repitition Range	Total Repitition Range	Optimal Repitition Range
< 70%	3 – 6	18 - 30	24
70 bis 79%	3 – 6	12 - 24	18
80 bis 89%	2 – 4	10 - 20	15
>89%	1 – 2	4 - 10	7

What is the purpose of the Prilepin table?

With this table, one can find his optimal repetition range for a certain intensity range. There is always a minimum and maximum number of repetitions to do per workout. If you do not do enough, then you do not progress, because there are too few stimuli. If you do too many repetitions, you may not be able to make any progress, because there are too many stimuli and the body can not recover enough.

The optimal range is the best ratio between time spent (repetitions made) and recovery.

Example:

Let's say you want to work out with 70% of your maximum weight. Then you should use the following sentence schema. 6 repetitions in 3 sentences. This corresponds exactly to the optimum range of 18 repetitions.

Important: The Prilepin table always refers to an exercise.

How to apply the Prilepin table for different intensity ranges?

Now you can combine the table for different intensity ranges and calculate how exhausting a workout is or how exhausting a whole week is. There are now different values that you should consider and with which you can periodize your own plan. High volume -> many stimuli -> recovery could be impaired. After the calculation one speaks of INOL. Here are the corresponding values.

Weekly INOL guidelines:

<2 easy, doable, good to do after exhausting weeks and preparation

2-3 tough, but doable, good for between rising stages

3-4 brutal, a lot of fatigue, good for a limited time and shock microcycles

> 4 Are you crazy?

Single Workouts INOL of a single exercise:

Workout INOL guidelines

<0.4 too few repetitions, not enough stimulus?

0.4-1 fresh, well done and optimal if you do not accumulate fatigue

1-2 hard, but good for loading phases

> 2 brutal

Now we come to the calculation of INOL.

INOL = Intensity Number of Lifts

Repetitions * sentences / (100 - intensity) = INOL

Example: Squat 5 reps, 3 sets in the intensity range of 75% in a workout.

5 * 3 / (100 - 75) = 0.6 INOL

This value is good according to the above guidelines and you do not have too much fatigue. Now if you do the workout 3 times a week. This results in a value of 1.8 INOL. Which corresponds to a light week. As a recovery week and at the same time make progress, this is a good value. In the longer term you should also switch to the higher INOL values to make further progress or to periodize your plan.

Example periodization:

Week 1 an area <2

Week 2 a range 2-3

Week 3 an area 3-4

Week 4 a range <2 (from here increase the weight)

Who invented the Prilepin Table?

Alexander Prilepin has immortalized his experience as a national coach in weightlifting in this table. Therefore, these values and experiences are based on top athletes trained by Alexander Prilepin in his work. But a recommendation from the weight lifting out therefore does not necessarily have to be optimal for the Powerlifting. Nevertheless, the Westside Barbell uses this principle. Whether it is just as acceptable for recreational athletes, put it there. But a test would be worth it.

RUSSIAN COMPLEX SENTENCES

Overview of the plan

Example squat

200kg 1 Rep

Maximum power set with 100% = 1 Rep 200kg

3-5 min. pause

Quick set with 50% 5 Rep with 100kg

3-5 min. pause

Maximum power set with 100% = 1 Rep 200kg

3-5 min. pause

Quick set with 50% 5 Rep with 100kg

3-5 min. pause

Maximum power set with 100% = 1 Rep 200kg

3-5 min. pause

Quick set with 50% 5 Rep with 100kg

3-5 min. pause

Maximum power set with 100% = 1 Rep 200kg

3-5 min. pause

Quick set with 50% 5 Rep with 100kg

3-5 min. pause

Maximum power set with 100% = 1 Rep 200kg

3-5 min. pause

Quick set with 50% 5 Rep with 100kg

Monday: legs (squats)
Tuesday: chest (bench press)
Wednesday: back (deadlift)
Thursday: Free
Friday: legs (squats)
Saturday: chest (bench press)
Sunday: back (deadlift)
Monday: Free

Planning

The plan can not be divided into blocks or similar. The scheme thus continues and there is no peak for, for example, a competition.

Periodization

A direct periodization is not available. From week to week the weight should be increased. Therefore it is a linear progression. Only it will be difficult to start with 100% weight, from there to increase.

As a modification you could go instead of 100% in the direction of 95%. Thus, the weight could be increased over the weeks longer.

Programming

Differences are not specified according to the plan. The intensity remains constant, one training day and the week.

To apply the plan is only the basic disciplines. Variations are also not further specified and must be added at their discretion.

The volume tends to be low. Weights below 60% can not be counted as volume in terms of powerlifting training.

Specification

Because only the competition exercises are given, one might think that the program is very specific. Only the quick power sets have only a small influence on the maximum force. In powerlifting, it does not matter how fast you move a weight. It just has to be moved.

The volume above 80% is very low in the competition exercises. Rather, the competition practice is trained with high intensity. This is 100% but very high and not practical, even if in powerlifting it is only about the maximum force.

Overload

The plan is based on percentage calculations. It is burdened with heavy weights from the beginning. The volume and intensity remains constant.

Fatigue management

A fatigue management is not available. It is heard on the body and accordingly reduces the number of sentences. A maximum of 5 heavy sentences are carried out. If you have a bad day, reduce it to, for example, 3 heavy sets and, accordingly, the quick power sets.

Individual differences

Individual differences are not discussed. Volume and intensity are the same for everyone in the plan. Further exercise selection is not specified.

Due to the high intensity, the maximum force is reached quickly. But not beyond, as the possibility of increases is very difficult.

Conclusion

As a complete training plan, the Russian complex sentences can not be designated. It is more of a scheme to put a new stimulus in training for a short time, unless you follow a training plan.

Also not recommended for competition preparation as there is no peak in the plan. Means it starts immediately with maximum weights and no slow increase towards the competition. There is a possibility of burnout.

The volume is too low and the intensity too high. A certain autoregulation is present, in that it should be 3-5 complex sentences.

For a little training shock it would be an idea.

SHEIKO ROUTINE

This is about Sheiko routines # 29, # 30, # 31, # 32.

Boris Sheiko, the inventor of these routines, is one of Russia's best-known Russian coaches. He has coached various record holders and champions like Andrey Belyaev, Kirill Sarychev or Yuri Fedorenko. Through his successful athletes and his approach of high volumes in training, his plans and he became famous.

Background of his plans

His plans came about through science and practical experience with eastern weightlifters. By training his athletes for decades and using his information, he has spawned some world-class athletes.

The routines have been translated from English into his book with the help of tools and some users have rebuilt these plans. The plans are just examples and Sheiko never thought that these plans should be used as a "copied version". Each of his athletes gets a plan tailored to their needs.

Now every plan goes over a month and all the plans are related and a 16 week peaking cycle is created. (Peaking = training for a competition in the top, moving maximum weights). We will not evaluate the plans as examples, but as stipulated guidelines.

Sheiko program analysis

Analyzing your program is difficult, because every training block has a slightly different design. You can download here the Sheiko plans as Excel format.

Download Sheiko program

Some basic features are that is always trained 3 times a week. Generally speaking, Bank is trained every day, flexing Monday and Friday, deadlifts are always on Wednesdays.

Every training day is quite high in the training volume. 200 to 400 repetitions per week over 50% intensity.

Planning

The sixteen week cycle we look at is broken down into four blocks: # 29, # 30, # 31, and # 32. Very loose, in structure, I would label them as follows:

29: Preparation block; Medium Volume - Medium Intensity

30: accumulation block: high volume - medium intensity

31: Transmutation block: medium volume - medium intensity

32: Realization / Peaking Block: Low Volume - High Intensity

29: Preparation block: As you can see, every 4 weeks are relatively equal in volume. But if you look more closely, you realize that the first 2 weeks do not go over 80%. Background is simple, that the athlete should get used to the high volume slowly. At the end of this block, the athlete is introduced to the right loads of Sheiko.

30: accumulation block: No work is done above 90% intensity but compared to # 29, 50% more total volume in the first week. The first week is brutal, then in week 2 the volume is reduced and no repetitions over 80% are made. Week 3 will be even harder than Week 1. Thereafter, Week 4 is almost a Deload, as volume is drastically reduced. The variation in volume and intensity makes the program feasible.

31: Transmutation Block: Now you will notice that this part of the plan is trained with semi heavy work over 90%. It also has a lot more work over 80% than the blocks before. The volume was also greatly reduced. Why is this done? This block is designed to slowly prepare you for the peak, slowly increasing the intensity and decreasing the volume. As a result, you recover from the volume and slowly get used to heavy weights coming in the next block.

32: Realization / Peaking Block: This block is used for direct preparation for heavy weights or competitions. But this block is also useless without the previous blocks. The volume is drastically reduced and the work over 90% is maintained. Week 2 is actually the only real week of training. Weeks 3 and 4 are used as deload and recreation for the # 30 and # 31. This block is used as "realization" for maximum weights. These should now be able to be shown on a competition.

This plan was planned for real powerlifters training for a competition. The plan uses advanced compensation principles to get the best performance in week 16.

Periodization

The periodization is not laid as in the classical sense with a focus on muscle growth, strength and speed, but on the individual disciplines such as bench press, deadlift or squat. Here also the volume is changed from week to week of the individual disciplines.

This is a smart way to periodize for the later stages for advanced or elite powerlifters. It is likely that you will not be able to simultaneously increase all disciplines because the total volume, the ability to recover, will surpass. Thus, the total amount at each lift will be quite varied.

In # 29, deadlifting is preferred and less bench presses are used to squat. In # 30, the squat volume and bench volume is dramatically increased by about 50%. The deadlift volume, however, is only increased by 10%. In # 31, squat volume is further increased to a level almost double that of the deadlift. # 32, in terms of volume, it is fairly balanced, because the volume is low for all three disciplines, in order to come for a competition in the top.

Programming

Not only does Sheiko show significant differences in volume from session to session and week to week, but you can also see it with significant variations from block to block! This makes Sheiko the most modern program we have seen so far.

Primarily I would say this plan is for advanced or elite powerlifters. For beginners and early advanced, this plan is not very effective, because the weight is increased only slowly.

Specification

Sheiko actually did carry out the vast majority of the volume through the competitive moves. For Sheiko, the movements are performed at regular intervals: three times a week for the bench, twice a week for the squat and once a week for the deadlift. Sheiko is actually a program that is explicitly designed for the purpose of powerlifting. Sheiko is a powerlifting program through and through.

There are a few criticisms points. First and foremost, due to the extremely high bandwidth of the program, the average amount of work done is low. This is done so that lifters can survive the volume. The average intensity on Sheiko, for each movement, is usually below 70%. During programs, you rarely, if ever, go above 90%. In fact, for the bench press, you do not go above 90% by week 10. In my opinion, the program could be improved by reducing the overall volume and increasing the average intensity.

Maybe the biggest problem with Sheiko is that it's a bit too specific. This means that with every single lift per session, the less you can get out of it. As an example, if you let yourself tan over and over again for 15 minutes, you will become less and less brown from each session. The same kind of effect happens when you only do the competitive moves.

Maybe a few numbers examples. You get 100% of the competition squats, only 80% of the second training session and only 60% of the third training week in the third training session. Well, if instead of the third unit, for example, inserted paused flexion, then you would eventually get 75% transfer to the competition squat, which is significantly more than 60%. That means you need variation in the disciplines.

Overload

Sheiko is based on percentage calculations. You start with the last known maximum weight competition and the whole cycle is calculated from that number. The progression works through basic overload. The lifter lifts heavier weights and more volume over time so that the cycle culminates in the week 16 with new bests.

Fatigue management

Sheiko does a great job at fatigue management. It changes volume and intensity from session to session, week to week and from block to block. Extremely difficult units are always followed by lighter units.

Likewise, the total frequency of # 29, # 30, # 31, and # 32 largely limits fatigue. While a unit takes a long time, you only train three times a week. In general, you only do 2-3 exercises for the lower body and upper body of each workout. For most people this is possible.

In my opinion Sheiko has too much useless volume. In block # 29 you make twice as much volume as in the Texas method in the crook. Many older athletes already have problems with recovery there. What will Sheiko do first?

There is the minimum volume to keep progressing and the maximum volume you can recover from. Somewhere in between is the optimal area.

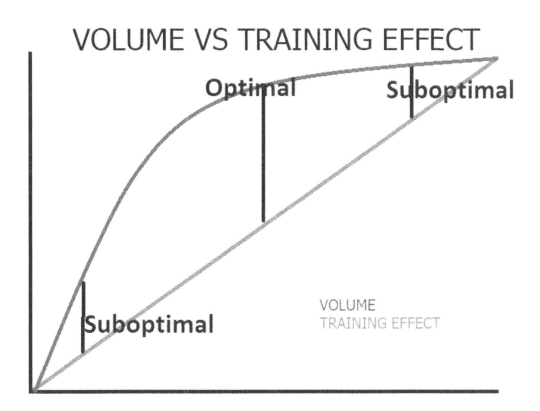

The goal is to have the most area under the curve. There, the ratio between time and volume is best.

Of course you can also train with more volume. But in order to make progress in the long term, one must constantly increase the volume. Only if you train too early with high volume and adapt to it, you have to train super high volume to make progress. The time required will be immensely in an early stage.

There is no need for such a high volume as you progress.

Individual differences

Well Sheiko ignores completely individual differences completely.

The maximum power is only increased at the end of a cycle. If the force improves during the cycle, you will still be able to stay at about 60% intensity most of the time. That is not optimal.

A far more important point is that volume is not autoregulated. Everyone needs a different volume. For many, this high volume can be too much and you get worse.

But to stay fair. Sheiko never wanted to write a program that anyone could just copy and train for. Each athlete is individually cared for by Sheiko.

Conclusion

The plan is one of the best plans for powerlifters ever described here. But not optimal. It lacks volume autoregulation and adapting to individual differences. A copied plan will never bring the perfect results either.

For advanced or elite powerlifters it would be a good plan to test. You can also jump to the "MSIC plans". If you do not make any further progress, you can of course contact Sheiko personally to get coached by him. He has produced very strong raw powerlifters.

Sheiko is suboptimal in my opinion. The volume is too high for some people, the intensity is a bit too low for my taste. There is a slight lack of variation and, above all, there is no autoregulation. Without autoregulation, I do not believe that a program for intermediate or advanced athletes can be optimal.

SMOLOV SQUAT CYCLE

Smolov can be roughly divided into five mesocycles:

1) Introduction phase - Preparation block

2) Base phase - accumulation block

3) "switching phase" - transition block

4) "Intensive" phase - transmutation block

5) "Peak" phase - hit realization block / peak

introductory phase

	Monday	Wednesday	Friday
Week 1	3x8@65%	3x8@65%	4x5@70%
	5@70%	5@70%	3@75%
	2x2@75%	2x2@75%	2x2@80%
	1@80%	1@80%	1@90%
Week 2	2x2@85%	3@85%	5@85%

Scheme sets x repetitions @ intensity

Through the introductory phase, the body should slowly get used to the frequency and the volume. In week 1, we will work up to a single of 90%. In Week 2, 5 repetitions of 85% are worked up. There are a few that skip the introductory phase. But if you have not had any experience with Smolov or have generally had less frequency and volume in training, then you should do the introductory phase.

Base phase - accumulation block

	Monday	Wednesday	Fiday	Saturday
Week 1	4x9@70%	5x7@75%	7x5@80%	10x3@85%
Week 2	4x9@70%	5x7@75%	7x5@80%	10x3@85%
	+10kg	+10kg	+10kg	+10kg
Week 3	4x9@70%	5x7@75%	7x5@80%	10x3@85%

	+15kg	+15kg	+15kg	+15kg
Week 4	Rest	Rest	Test 1RM	

Scheme sets x repetitions @ intensity

After the introductory phase, you enter the high-volume rage that is the "basic mescocycle". In the base phase it gets exciting. You train 4 times a week in the squat. Each workout is done more than 30 repetitions. At the end of each week you have to do ten triples at 85%. That is really crazy.

It does not get easier from week to week! In week 2 you have to increase by 10 kilos. In week 3, another 5 kilos, so that you used the same training scheme as in week 1 but increased your weight by 15 kilos. Is it any wonder that this program leads to amazing progress for those who can survive?

"Switching phase" - transition block

	Monday	Wednesday	Friday
Week 1	Squat negative	Power Clean	Box Squat
	1@105%	8x3@60%	12x2@60%
	1@110%	8x3@65%	12x2@65%

Scheme sets x repetitions @ intensity

The switching phase is essentially a transition block. In this block alternative exercises are trained and speed trained. But it's not so much about whether the athlete actually gets faster or not. But the athlete should recover from the brutality of the base phase and put even slight stimuli. You should do this week as you definitely need a rest.

"Intensive" phase - transmutation block

	Monday	Wednesday	Friday
Week 1	3@65%	3@60%	4@65%
	4@75%	3@70%	4@70%
	3x4@85%	4@80%	5x4@80%
	5@85%	3@90%	
		2x5@85%	
Week 2	4@60%	3@65%	3@65%
	4@70%	3@75%	3@75%
	4@80%	3@85%	4@85%
	3@90%	3x3@90%	4x5@90
	2x4@90%	3@95%	
Week 3	3@60%	3@60%	3@65%
	3@70%	3@70%	3@75%
	3@80%	3@80%	3@85%
	5x5@90%	2x3@95%	4x3@95
Week 4	3@70%	3@70%	3@75%
	4@80%	3@80%	4@90%
	5x5@90%	4x3@95%	3x4@95
Week 5	4@75%		Test 1RM
	4x4@85%		

Scheme sets x repetitions @ intensity

After the basic work done from the base phase, the Intensive Phase helps you to turn the gains into maximum power.

This is an absolutely brutal mesocycle. It is trained only 3 times a week but the intensity is extremely high. In the first week, you run 54 lifts over 80%, in the second week 54 lifts over 80%, but 43 of them are over 90%! In the 3rd week 47 lifts over 80% but of them 18 over 95%. The fourth week is the craziest with

55 lifts over 80%, 48 lifts over 90% and 24 lifts over 95%. Needless to say, if you survive, you will be ready and prepared for huge excellence.

Planning

The final phase (week 5 of the intense phase) of Smolov is the competition preparation Taper.

As you can see, Smolov is brutal until the very end. Only in the last week of the program, you can rest a little. As the workload or volume decreases. But even the last phase is more intense than most programs you know. Especially from the western world.

Periodization

Smolov uses a rather complex periodization model.

The introductory microcycle primarily serves only to prepare the athlete for "real" phases of Smolov. The purpose here is just to get the athlete into higher frequencies and workloads. This is a classic preparation block.

The basal mesocycle targets primarily hypertrophy and total work capacity. There is one training per week with 85%, of which 10 triple. For example, the rest of the week deals with repetitions in the range of 70-80% and even goes up to nine repetitions. This part of the program is most conducive to mass gains through the chosen reps and intensity. In addition, the volume is massively increased and forms the basis for the intensive phase later in the program. If you can finish the base phase, you have a bit more muscle and built-up volume tolerance that will allow you to make huge profits during the intense phase and still be alive.

The switching phase is a classic transition block. Here the focus is on speed and alternative exercises. The velocity volume helps to maintain the central nervous system adjustments and to recover the body. And so to prepare for the intense phase.

After all, the intense phase is the part of bringing everything together. Here most of the work is done over 90% and the volume is reduced. This will end in massive bests.

Programming

Smolov uses a form of block programming.

The first weeks should prepare you for the massive loads during the basic mesocycle. The basic demo cycle itself is best understood as a volume / accumulation block.

The switching phase is a transition block. Here primarily the recovery is to be facilitated by unloading. This helps to contribute to the overall effect of the program.

Now in the intensive phase, the volume is reduced and the intensity increased. Here you will realize your gains in power. The intensity is incredibly high and most training volume goes over 90%.

Block programming model is suitable for advanced athletes.

Specification

Smolov is not a powerlifting program. Because the focus of this routine is on the squat. The program will not perform a deadlift, and those who are not used to such high volume will likely need to reduce their upper body workout. So that you can survive Smolov.

Smolov is not specific enough for powerlifting. Your total total is not trying to increase, but only the squat.

If you have a weak squat, seemingly reacting to nothing and making no progress. Then it is recommended to do a shock cycle like Smolov. However, it will probably affect your other lifts. If your goal is to increase your total, Smolov does not recommend.

One problem is the low variation. Only the competition squat will be trained. However, for each training day, one has a lower yield of the optimal result for the carry-over. With the first squat training one has a 100% yield with the second but only a 90% yield and so on sinking. Therefore, it would be better to train different squat variations.

It could be possible to achieve even better results with more squat variations, because one often gets a greater yield from "new" stimuli that the body is no match for. Frontsquat does not recommend it directly, although the carry is probably better than a third normal squat day.

Overload

Smolov uses a progressive overload. The weight on the base mesocycle is increased every week. During the intensive phase, the percentages are raised every week. Each week, the lift manages heavier loads for more reps and sets. Ergo, Smolov uses a basic progressive overload.

Fatigue management

The whole idea beyond Smolov is that it should act as a shock cycle. In other words, this program is literally designed to overwhelm you and make you flirt with overtraining.

Two types of fatigue are managed. First, no deadlift and no lower body exercises. Second, by implementing block programming. After the basic measurement cycle, for example, 2 weeks of recovery are planned.

However, many can not handle the program. And either they burn out or get hurt. Hardly anyone needs such a high volume. Always think about volume vs. Training effect.

It is neither necessary nor is it optimal to carry out such a routine. Most people lose part of their profits to Smolov. Why? To get more progress, the volume has to be increased. However, Smolov is already so brutal in volume that everything else in training plans has less volume and therefore some gains in strength go back.

Individual differences

Smolov does not go into individual differences at all. Smolov is a percentage shock cycle. It would not make sense to pay attention to individual differences. Why? Because if you tried to automatically regulate the training effect of a program like Smolov, you would end up making only a fraction of the total original volume.

If you are an advanced athlete and consider the plan, be aware that you are in a precarious position. You can only hope that you survive the program, do not give up or hurt yourself. If you come through, then you will certainly bring a new best.

Conclusion

Some think it is about to prove masculinity and that one should perform such a brutal program. I can understand that.

However, it is not optimal to make progress in powerlifting!

For beginners and advanced users it is completely unsuitable. Because you can achieve better results with any other program. Or. Return on investment.

As a middle or elite you have to weigh the benefits and risks of this program. You will not have to do a deadlift and you will probably have to lower your bench press volume. You may also lose your winnings after the cycle when you return to normal volume. Nothing to Smolov is very suitable for long-term progress.

So why even think about it? Maybe you have the chance to break a record on a championship. Then the plan would make sense to specialize and you would be in the books.

What about the others? Then follow a plan to make long-term progress. Do not be greedy for short-term and possibly unsustainable results. If you chase after a record, then it might make sense. In virtually every other case, as powerlifters who are interested in maximizing our total number, the program is neither worth the risks nor is it a smart way to make long-term progress.

EXTENDED RUSSIAN POWER ROUTINE 9 WEEKS

Overview of the plan

NOTE: The retry schedule for the attached table is

(Sets x repetitions x weight).

1RM	
Squat	240
Bench	165
Deadlift	285

Smallest increment	5

Monday — Sets*Reps

		Sets*Reps
Week 1	Squat	6x2x190
	Bench	6x3x130
Week 2	Squat	6x2x190
	Bench	6x4x130
Week 3	Squat	6x2x190
	Bench	6x5x130
Week 4	Squat	6x2x190
	Bench	6x6x130
Week 5	Squat	6x2x190
	Bench	5x5x140
Week 6	Squat	6x2x190
	Bench	4x4x150
Week 7	Squat	6x2x190
	Bench	3x3x155
Week 8	Squat	6x2x190
	Bench	2x2x165
Week 9	Squat	6x2x190
	Bench	1x1x175

Wednesday — Sets*Reps

		Sets*Reps
Week 1	Deadlift	6x3x230
Week 2	Deadlift	6x4x230
Week 3	Deadlift	6x5x230
Week 4	Deadlift	6x6x230
Week 5	Deadlift	5x5x240
Week 6	Deadlift	4x4x255
Week 7	Deadlift	3x3x270
Week 8	Deadlift	2x2x285
Week 9	Deadlift	1x1x300

Friday — Sets*Reps

		Sets*Reps
Week 1	Squat	6x3x190
	Bench	6x2x130
Week 2	Squat	6x4x190
	Bench	6x2x130
Week 3	Squat	6x5x190
	Bench	6x2x130
Week 4	Squat	6x6x190
	Bench	6x2x130
Week 5	Squat	5x5x205
	Bench	6x2x130
Week 6	Squat	4x4x215
	Bench	6x2x130
Week 7	Squat	3x3x230
	Bench	6x2x130
Week 8	Squat	2x2x240
	Bench	6x2x130
Week 9	Squat	1x1x250
	Bench	6x2x130

Tips: I don't do much of assistance work, but if you have the energy after training, throw in some assistance work (lats, dips, shoulder presses etc.)

If you are a sumo deadlifter, start the cycle with traditional deadlift. At fifth week replace traditional deadlift with sumo deadlift.

It also gives the plan in a 6 week cycle. At the end, I will show him. I just want to talk about the 9 week plan. The plan probably originated from "USSR Yearbook Squat Routines 1974 and 1976 Spreadsheets".

Planning

As with Sheiko, you can divide the plan into 4 blocks. The plan is wonderful to use for a competition preparation.

Week 1-2: Preparation block; Medium Volume - Medium Intensity

Week 3-5: accumulation block: high volume - medium intensity

Week 6-7: Transmutation block: medium volume - medium intensity

Weeks 8-9: Realization / Peaking Block: Low Volume - High Intensity

Week 1-2: Preparation block: As you can see, the volume is slowly increasing. The first 2 weeks are not over 80% trained. Background is simple, that the athlete should get used to the high volume slowly.

Week 3-5: Accumulation block: Training up to 85% intensity. The total volume will be further increased during week 3 to 4. In week 5, the intensity is increased to 85% and the volume is reduced. Weeks 4 and 5 will be brutal but important for the rest of the week. You should not have any difficulty here, otherwise the weight is too heavy, which was chosen.

Week 6-7: Transmutation Block: Now you will notice that this part of the plan is trained with semi-heavy work over 90%. Much of the work is over 90% as the blocks before it. The volume has also been greatly reduced and continues to reduce. This part should prepare you slowly for the peak, in which the intensity is increased again and reduces the volume. The volume above 90% is higher than other plans.

Week 8-9: Realization / Peaking Block: This block is used as a direct preparation for heavy weights or competitions. Without the blocks or weeks before this block, this would be meaningless and not feasible. The volume is drastically reduced and the work over 100%. This block is used as a "realization" or test of the new maximum weights. If the plan is used as a preparation, you now have the choice. Either week 9, the last week of training and then it is paused or week 9 is canceled and used as a rest. Both work,

This plan was designed for real powerlifters training for a competition.

Periodization

Again, the periodization is not laid down in the classical sense with a focus on muscle growth, strength and speed, but on the individual disciplines.

In general, the bench press and the squat are preferred here. The volume runs parallel in both exercises. The increase is the same for all three disciplines.

Programming

It can be seen that there are large differences in the volume and intensity of the individual blocks. Unfortunately, there are no variations of the exercises.

Primarily I would say this plan is for early advanced or advanced. Because this plan increases the weight quite quickly. But you should still be familiar with heavy weights.

Specification

The focus is completely on the 3 disciplines. Other variations do not occur. It is only the volume made by the competition exercises. Twice a week for squat and bench press, deadlift only occurs once a week.

As a criticism, I would say that the plan is too specific. There is no training work below 70% or to build muscle. And that there are no variations in the plan.

If you train the same over and over again, then the effect you draw from it will be less and less.

For me, the upper body, according to the bench press trained too little. Here it should be supplemented by another variation.

Overload

Extended Russian Power Routine is based on percentage calculations. The last maximum weights are entered into the computer and the entire plan is automatically calculated. At the end of the week, new bests should be done.

Fatigue management

During the training weeks a lot of fatigue is collected. There are no deloads or recovery periods between weeks. Each week or block becomes exhausting in other ways.

The volume coupled with high intensity in recent weeks, will require a lot of recovery from the body.

Individual differences

Individual differences are completely ignored. The volume is not autoregulated and everyone needs a different volume. For one, the volume may be too little, for the other again suitable. For example, I had added an extra crest lifting tag and shoulder presses on Wednesday.

Conclusion

This plan is very good for powerlifters. Nevertheless, he is not optimal. There is a lack of volume autoregulation and adaptation to individual differences. Partly too specific as there are no variations.

The intensity may be a bit too high and the volume feasible. If you are already an Elite Powerlifter or well advanced, I would not recommend the plan. Because the weight is increased very quickly and also a lot of work over 80% is made.

For early advanced you can recommend the plan. With some own work one could adapt the plan even further and install variations.

Here is the plan for 6 weeks.

Sets)	Exercise 1RM	Squat 100	Bench 100	Deadlift 100
Week 1	Day 1	Day 2	Day 3
Squat	80x2 x6	80x3 x6	80x2 x6
Bench	80x3 x6	80x2 x6	80x4 x6
Deadlift	80x3 x6	80x2 x6	80x4 x6
Back Extension	6x2	6x3	6x4
Week 2	Day 1	Day 2	Day 3
Squat	80x4 x6	80x2 x6	80x5 x6
Bench	80x2 x6	80x5 x6	80x2 x6
Deadlift	80x2 x6	80x5 x6	80x2 x6
Back Extension	6x 5x	6x 6x	+5kg x6 x2
Week 3	Day 1	Day 2	Day 3
Squat	80x2 x6	80x6 x6	80x2 x6
Bench	80x6 x6	80x2 x6	85x5 x5
Deadlift	80x6 x6	80x2 x6	85x5 x5
Back Extension	+5kg x6 x3	+5kg x6 x4	+5kg x6 x5
Week 4	Day 1	Day 2	Day 3
Squat	85x5 x5	80x2 x6	90x4 x4
Bench	80x2 x6	90x4 x4	80x2 x6
Deadlift	80x2 x6	90x4 x4	80x2 x6
Back Extension	+5kg x6 x6	+10kg x6 x2	+10kg x6 x3
Week 5	Day 1	Day 2	Day 3
Squat	80x2 x6	95x3 x3	80x2 x6
Bench	95x3 x3	80x2 x6	100x2 x2
Deadlift	95x3 x3	80x2 x6	100x2 x2
Back Extension	+10kg x6 x4	+10kg x6 x5	+10kg x6 x6
Week 6	Day 1	Day 2	Day 3
Squat	100x2 x2	80x2 x6	110x1 or 105x1
Bench	80x2 x6	110x1	-
Deadlift	80x2 x6	110x1	-
Back Extension	+12kg x6 x2	+12kg x6 x3	+12kg x6 x4

BULGARIAN METHOD FOR POWERLIFTING

An exemplary Bulgarian program for powerlifting.

The Bulgarian method is less a set program than a collection of principles. You have to apply this yourself for your training.

Here is a simplified version of these principles:

1) up to a daily maximum for the squat and bench press

2) a few backoff sets with double or triple sets

3) Do not force repetitions and do not use "psyche-up" techniques

4) Deadlift once or twice a week - especially with a focus on speed work

5) Even if you feel like shit, you have to work out

6) a light week every 2-4 weeks - halve the volume, not more than 80%

Let's take a look at a hypothetical example of the Bulgarian method taken from Perryman's ideas:

Week	Monday	Tuesday	Wednesday	Thursday	Friday	Saturday
1	Squat ZM, BO x3 Bench ZM, BO x3 Chinups	Squat ZM, BO x2 Bench ZM, BO x2 Pullups	Frontsquat ZM, BO x3 Close Bench ZM, BO x3 Deadlift 2x10@70%	Squat ZM, BO x1 Bench ZM, BO x1 Chinups	Frontbow ZM, BO x2 Close Bench ZM, BO x2 Pullups	Deadlift ZM x3 Military Press ZM, BO x3 Row
2	Squat ZM, BO x3 Bench ZM, BO x3 Chinups	Squat ZM, BO x2 Bench ZM, BO x2 Pullups	Frontsquat ZM, BO x3 Close Bench ZM, BO x2 Deadlift 1x10@80%	Squat ZM, BO x1 Bench ZM, BO x1 Chinups	Frontsquat ZM, BO x1 Close Bench ZM, BO x1 Pullups	Deadlift ZM Military Press ZM, BO x2 Row
3	Deload, Volume bisect, not more than 80%					

ZM = the daily maximum

BO = backoff sentences

X3 = backoff triples

X2 = Backoff Doubles

X1 = backoff singles

Repetitions x sentences

Periodization

There are no times that focus on different muscular qualities. The plan will focus on singles all the time. Occasionally, Abadjiev (inventor of the plan) occasionally has his lifts in parts of the off-season make more hypertrophy-oriented repetitions.

Advanced athletes have the problem that they need more and more volume to progress. Therefore, they have two options, either they can periodize or they can improve their recovery. The Bulgarian method is unique in that it gives the athlete the opportunity to master absolutely crazy volume over time.

This is the reason why more advanced periodization is not required here. It is simply worth increasing the work capacity over time.

Programming

Some Olympic coaches are different in their plan. You choose the backoff sets as you wish while using the Bulgarian method. Everything is determined by the feeling. In a way, that's not really programming. But it is not the best idea to train everything for feeling. Therefore, a certain structure is needed.

In the plan itself, a Deload week is recommended every 2 weeks. Thus, the total work is screwed down and you can recover.

However, most of the programmatic variation of the Bulgarian method is determined by your fatigue. On days when you're fine, you'll do more and just the opposite will happen if you're not feeling well.

As a result, the volume is autoregulated from week to week and the volume itself changes in the plan itself. It is suitable for advanced athletes as the emphasis is on increasing work ability. Intelligent unloading protocols should also be used.

A beginner could use the plan with the help of a coach and less frequency. Without it is difficult for the beginner to use autoregulation, as he simply lacks the experience.

Specification

I have to criticize that the Bulgarian method is too specific. Let me explain that. The law of accommodation "law of accommodation" states that the more often the body is exposed to the same stimulus, the less the body will show adaptive response (adaptation). This applies to a large extent to the choice of movement and to a lesser extent to the training intensity.

In the original version of the Bulgarian method, you do only a handful of exercises, and these usually singles. Let us expect a little to illustrate the law a little bit.

Let's take the squat. In the first training you will get 100% as return on investment. The 2nd training maybe 80%, the 3rd 60% and the 4th training maybe 40%. Well, if, for example, a paused squat is done, then the carry will be 75%. This means that if you use paused squat as 3rd training, you will end up with more carry over or more adjustment. Thus, get more results for the time invested.

The plan was originally developed and tested for the Olympic weightlifting. There is very little information related to powerlifting and so you have to test yourself a lot. This can be a disadvantage, but it does not have to be. Other methods of powerlifting are far more sophisticated and offer less chance of errors and stagnation.

Overload

The plan uses a progressive overload to progress. You should be able to increase your daily maximum weight over time. Of course, this is only possible if you can increase your weights every week. Heavy weights are more likely to progress.

The volume is automatically regulated and increases slowly. This leads to further progress. As the body has to adapt to the increasing volume, which it has not mastered before.

Fatigue management

One point of criticism would be that many follow the Bulgarian method. without you really need the volume. Most weightlifters who followed this plan had been through years of training and could slowly train their work capacity there.

You can certainly jump straight into the plan, then you will probably have a problem, in terms of long-term development. How so? ? There are two main reasons:

1) You have nowhere more volume after this program

2) There is an optimal dose-response relationship between volume and adaptive adaptation

Let me explain the first problem a bit. Let's say you jump straight into the plan and squat 6 times a week. Now you come to a plateau. What do you want to do now? The Bulgarians did the following, they trained twice a day and later extended their training times. Do you have the time for that? Then you have few options to increase the volume or the frequency.

Well I think this plan will short-term long-term gains. Let me explain it. Each training represents an adaptation cycle. The volume of a training session determines the size of the adaptation response.

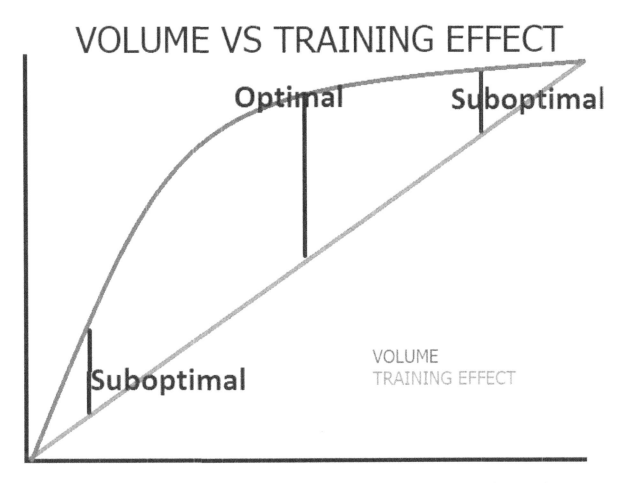

As you can see, the more volume you make in a session, the bigger the answer will be. Likewise, the less volume you have in a session, the less the answer will be. Why should you do little volume per workout? Well, you can recover faster from that and drive a higher frequency. That is exactly what the Bulgarian method does. Unlike Sheiko or Smolov, there is high volume per session performed.

Now both methods lead to success. Our goal as a lifter, however, is to bring our volume as far as possible under the adjustment curve. We want to have the largest distance between the volume curve and the fitting curve. Because there we have the biggest return on investment. If you work with a lot of volume per workout then you will have less return on investment.

The body has an ultimate limit to the volume that it can handle and you only have a limited amount of time to work out, so the person will have a better overall performance that has the greater return on investment per session.

The person driving super high volume will reach the limits faster and not get as much benefit per stress recovery and adjustment cycle.

Now the same problem can occur even with a small volume per workout. You'll go through more recovery, adjustment, and stress cycles, but if you train to the same volume as one who works with the optimal volume, your performance will still be lower.

For example, if the optimal volume per workout is 500 kilos for you, and the total weekly volume you can recover from is 1500 kilos, what should be your frequency? Well, it should be three times a week (1500/500 = 3).

Now you can easily complete the volume in a single training session or spread it over six 250 kilo sessions. Both approaches have exactly the same volume but the problem is the lower overall adjustment. The reason is, you are too far from the optimal dose of exercise stress.

Now high-frequency training can also be a necessity for advanced athletes. As an an example. 7000 kilos per week and 1000 kilos per training, from which he can recover. Then the bill would be 7000/1000 = 7 training days.

Now in the real world, this is a complex question. Because the numbers are never so easy and it's difficult to know when to get more frequency.

For advanced athletes there will come a time and he will have the need of more frequency. For a beginner this will probably work, but this is suboptimal.

Individual differences

Unlike other programs we have looked at here, the Bulgarian method is fully autoregulated. If you work your way up to the daily maximum weight, then it will be determined by your day shape and motivation.

Furthermore, a time limit of training and the rule of not performing forced repetitions, further limiting the volume and auto-regulating. These ideas are from Perryman.

The time limit means if you have set a training timeout, then you will stop using the backoff sets beforehand if you run out of time.

Most errors are often caused by the athlete himself and are not a mistake of the Bulgarian method. A competent coach chooses the right frequency according to the training progress of the athlete. It is strongly recommended to slowly increase the frequency and volume. The Bulgarian coach Abadjiev taught his athletes that through years of hard training.

Conclusion

I think such a plan as the Bulgarian method should be the ultimate goal of an advanced powerlifter. The more volume you need, the more frequency you have to use to keep making progress. But only if you want to do a life-long best.

Beginners should not be blinded by the successes of the Bulgarians. These have taken years to use such a frequency and to bring such success. Therefore, the plan is not intended for beginners.

In short, the Bulgarian method is a fantastic, highly intelligent way to train, provided you are qualified to train like that. Most of you just are not. Therefore, do not choose the shortcut if you are not ready yet and train yourself long term.

Imprint:

https://www.powerliftingcheck.de

© 2020 Randy Bolz

Sterndamm 17

12487 Berlin

Edition (1)

Cover design, illustration: Randy Bolz

Editing, proofreading: Randy Bolz

Translation: Randy Bolz

Editor: Randy Bolz

Printer: Amazon Europe in Luxembourg

The work including its parts is protected by copyright. Any use is prohibited without the consent of the publisher and the author. This applies in particular to electronic or other duplication, translation, distribution and public disclosure.

Source:

Mark Rippetoe Starting Strength

powerliftingtowin

Made in the USA
Coppell, TX
21 March 2023